Let Us Go Over to
Bethlehem

A Guide to the Moravian Community

The Rev. Dr. Douglas W. Caldwell
The Rev. Carol A. Reifinger

Central Moravian Church
Bethlehem, Pennsylvania

ISBN 0-9711797-2-7

Printed in the United States of America
by
Chernay Printing, Inc.
Coopersburg, Pennsylvania
2007

Let Us Go Over to
Bethlehem

Table of Contents

Foreword

The Bible reminds us that on a particular night long ago in the Middle East, a group of shepherds were going about their normal routine of tending a herd of sheep. The usual night noises of those rustling sheep, perhaps some crickets, or a puff of wind were suddenly disturbed by the extraterrestrial sound of an angel's voice, surrounded by a brilliant illumination. It told those frightened shepherds about the birth of a baby in a small community called Bethlehem. This Child was a Savior, Christ the Lord. Then a great number of angels appeared to them singing a song, "Glory to God in the highest and on earth peace, good will toward people."

After this unbelievable experience, the shepherds began to speak to one another and said, "Let us go over to Bethlehem and see this thing which is come to pass." And we are told that they left their sheep, their cares, their responsibilities and made a pilgrimage to Bethlehem and discovered Mary and Joseph and the new born baby lying in a manger.

You, too, have made a pilgrimage to another Bethlehem. It is a community founded by yet other pilgrim people from Europe called "The Moravians."

Now that you are here, we want your visit to be one of discovery, meaning, fulfillment and wonder. We have written this guide book to assist you in your venture.

It is intended to be an enjoyable book as we share anecdotes, a bit of history, and interesting insights about a church and community we have come to personally appreciate and love.

Perhaps after your sojourn with us, your life may be inspired and even blessed. You, too, may find that as you leave us and return to your home, that you will also, in your own way, find that you are "glorifying and praising God for all the things that you have heard and seen."

Douglas W. Caldwell
Carol A. Reifinger
Fall 2007

v

Some Facts about Moravians and Bethlehem

- Bethlehem was founded on Christmas Eve 1741.
- The **first place of worship** was the Saal of the Gemeinhaus, now the Moravian Museum.
- The 1751 Old Chapel was the **second place of worship.**
- The **third place of worship** is Central Moravian Church, built in 1803 – 1806.
- The Bell House and Sisters' House are still used as private residences.
- The Bach Choir performs regularly in Central Moravian Church in the *Bach at Noon* series.
- Moravian Academy shares the Central Moravian Church campus for its Lower and Middle Schools.
- The Historic Bethlehem Partnership, Inc. was founded in 1993 to coordinate the museums and other historic sites.

How the worldwide Moravian Church is organized:

There are 19 Provinces around the world.
Bethlehem, PA is in the Northern Province, Eastern District.

Some Statistics for the Moravian Church:

45,000 members in North America
600,000 members in Africa
30,000 members in Europe
    (including Great Britain)

Moravian Churches in Bethlehem, PA:

Advent Moravian Church
Central Moravian Church
College Hill Moravian Church
East Hills Moravian Church
Edgeboro Moravian Church
West Side Moravian Church

Total membership of all 6 Bethlehem churches is about 3300.

❖ The Moravian Church is a modern day Protestant denomination.

❖ The earliest roots of the church in the 1400's go back to the Czech Republic, and in the 1700's to Germany.

To learn about the history of the Moravian Church, we begin with a glimpse at the life stories and witness of three significant people: a priest, an educator and a nobleman.

John Hus

The Roman Catholic priest, John Hus, is considered the 'spiritual father' of the Moravian Church, known as the *Unitas Fratrum*, or Unity of the Brethren. Hus lived in Prague in the 1400's, in what is now the Czech Republic. His ministry included teaching at the university and preaching in the Bethlehem Chapel in Prague.

A popular preacher, Hus promoted the idea of the reading of scripture and preaching in the native language, instead of in Latin, during worship. He encouraged congregational singing.

Struggling with what he felt were inappropriate practices of church leaders of his day, Hus began speaking out against the financial and moral corruption of his fellow priests.

Some 100 years before Martin Luther came on the scene, Hus' bold statements and teachings led to a strong reaction on the part of the Catholic Church. After an ecclesiastical trial, at which he was branded unjustly as a heretic, he was burned at the stake on July 6, 1415.

Followers of Hus were persecuted and some of them went into hiding in order to worship according to the beliefs that they shared. Not far from Prague, they met and worshipped in secret. In the year 1457, a new church, the *Unitas Fratrum*, gradually came into being, shaped by his convictions.

John Amos Comenius

Many years later, one of the most famous members of the *Unitas Fratrum* was Bishop John Amos Comenius. We refer to

1

him today as the "Father of Modern Education." Comenius wrote extensively and attempted to bring together in written form, all of the knowledge of the day. He pioneered the practice of including pictures in textbooks. Unlike many of his time, he believed in the education of girls as well as boys, because girls would one day become mothers and be responsible for the upbringing of the children.

Comenius suffered one tragic loss after another. His books were burned and he was persecuted in his homeland, so he and a small band of followers fled to Poland for refuge. His work took him to Sweden, England and the Netherlands, where he is buried.

Tradition has it that at one point Comenius was offered the first Presidency of Harvard University, but declined.

A large statue of Comenius stands on the Main Street campus of Moravian College.

Count Nikolaus Ludwig von Zinzendorf

After many years of worshipping in secret across Europe, some of those who had left Bohemia and Moravia because of religious persecution, as well as other refugees, settled in Germany in 1722, on the land of a Lutheran nobleman, Count Nikolaus Ludwig von Zinzendorf. With his permission, they built homes clustered in the new community called Herrnhut, or, "on watch for the Lord."

Difficulties soon arose within the new community. Differences in matters of faith and doctrine were troublesome. Zinzendorf began meeting with individuals within the community to speak and to pray with them.

At a service of Holy Communion on August 13, 1727, at the nearby Berthelsdorf Lutheran Church, these "Moravians" felt the stirrings of the Holy Spirit and a new willingness to reach out to one another. Seeing that they did not disperse after this powerful and emotional worship experience, Zinzendorf sent food from his manor house to homes around the community so that people could remain together in conversation. The gathering of people and the partaking of food together reminded him of the *agapē* or *lovefeast* meal of the ancient Christians. Eventually, the new community would gather for lovefeast for various occasions; simple meals shared in the context of a worship service. The practice of lovefeast continues to this day.

2

Following the spiritual experience at Berthelsdorf, old divisions were healed and a new zeal for mission to others began to take shape. The experience marked the Spiritual Birthday of the Renewed Moravian Church, now celebrated on the Sunday nearest August 13th.

A History of Missions

After returning from a visit to Copenhagen, Denmark, for the coronation of the Danish king, Zinzendorf spoke about a slave named Anthony that he met in the city. Anthony's story of the harsh treatment of his people on the island of St. Thomas in the Caribbean touched Zinzendorf and others deeply. Zinzendorf encouraged the Moravians to go to those who needed to hear the Gospel, wherever that might lead them.

As a result of his encouragement and the moving of the Spirit among the people of the community, Moravians began sending missionaries to other lands in 1732. The first missionaries traveled to the island of St. Thomas and lived quietly among the people. Gradually the outreach to other islands and countries began to grow and Moravian missions became a worldwide phenomenon.

The current list of countries in which Moravians have planted churches or fellowships includes: Costa Rica, the Eastern West Indies, Guyana, Honduras, Jamaica, Labrador, Nicaragua, South Africa, Suriname, Tanzania, Congo, French Guyana, Malawi and Zambia and various European countries, such as the Czech Republic, Germany, the Netherlands and Great Britain. Other mission areas include: Albania, Latvia and South Asia, which encompasses India, Tibet and Nepal.

A Mission Outreach of Central Moravian Church

One significant outreach effort in the modern day Moravian Church was initiated by Central Moravian Church in Bethlehem, PA. A partnership with the **Sikonge Moravian Church in Tanzania, East Africa** was established in 1990 as a direct result of the influence of the Rev. Eliah Kategile, who was studying at Moravian Theological Seminary at the time. He and his family encouraged Central Moravian Church to consider assisting the Sikonge Church in the building of a new sanctuary.

The sanctuary was built and an ongoing relationship was strengthened through the work of a husband and wife team of two retired physicians and members of Central Church, Dr. William Hoffman and Dr. Margaret Kraybill. The Hoffmans initiated the protocols now used throughout the country which provide medication for pregnant mothers to prevent the transmission of HIV/AIDS to their unborn children.

In their work in the Sikonge and Tabora regions of Tanzania, the Hoffmans soon discovered that a pressing problem was the **welfare of the orphans** who remained after their parents had died of AIDS. Typically, grandmothers cared for these children, but were often impoverished themselves and ill-equipped to take on child care responsibilities. An orphans' program, started by the Hoffmans and now run by a local woman, Mama Kimwaga, has helped feed and clothe and provide schooling for thousands of children.

On a trip to Sikonge in July of 2006, several Central Moravian Church members were interviewed and photographed as they visited villages along with the Hoffmans. A series in the *Morning Call* newspaper, called "One Faith, Two Worlds," chronicles their journey and experiences.

An outpouring of concern and money soon followed, as the Board of World Mission of the Moravian Church received many donations as a result of the publication of the series.

Today, the next chapter in the work of Central Moravian Church is waiting to be written, as the partnership with Sikonge continues to grow and change.

Children in the Orphans' Program in Sikonge, Tanzania, East Africa

What We Believe

Those who choose to join the Moravian Church sign the *Moravian Covenant for Christian Living*. The *Moravian Covenant* is a document that has its roots in the history of the early Herrnhut, Germany community. In 1727, Count Zinzendorf set forth some basic, practical means of living a Christian life for those who inhabited this new community. Originally, the document that he

created was called, "The Brotherly Agreement."
The title has been changed in recent times to be more inclusive.

The opening section of the *Covenant* now features the "Ground of Our Witness," a statement of faith that was not as explicit in the older forms of the document. We proclaim that we are called into a Christian fellowship by Christ. The source of our life and salvation is the God revealed to us in scripture. A specific Moravian confession of faith can be found in the Easter Liturgy of our Church, however, we also recognize and value the historic creeds of the Christian Church at large.

The other topics addressed in the *Moravian Covenant* are: The Witness of the Christian Life; The Witness of a Living Church; The Witness of the Christian Home; The Witness of a Christian Citizen; Our Witness in the World.

Our Hymns Declare Our Faith

In the *Moravian Book of Worship*, Count Zinzendorf is quoted as saying that the hymnal is a response to the Bible. In the Bible, we see how God speaks with people; and in the hymnal, how people speak with God.

Moravians have always had a great appreciation for music and a long history of hymn writing.

One of our beloved hymns, "Jesus Call Thou Me," is sung at the Christmas Eve Vigil services at Central Moravian Church as a traditional reminder of the founding of the community by Zinzendorf in 1741. The words of the hymn express our faith:

> *Not Jersualem –*
> *lowly Bethlehem*
> *'twas that gave us*
> *Christ to save us;*
> *not Jerusalem.*

The *Book of Worship* also preserves for us a hymn from the 15th century by John Hus, "Lord Jesus Christ, Our Salvation."

Zinzendorf was a prolific hymn writer and many of his hymns are printed in the *Book of Worship*, including "Christian Hearts, in Love United," and "Jesus, Still Lead On."

Moravian Motto
In essentials unity,
in non-essentials, liberty
and in all things love.

5

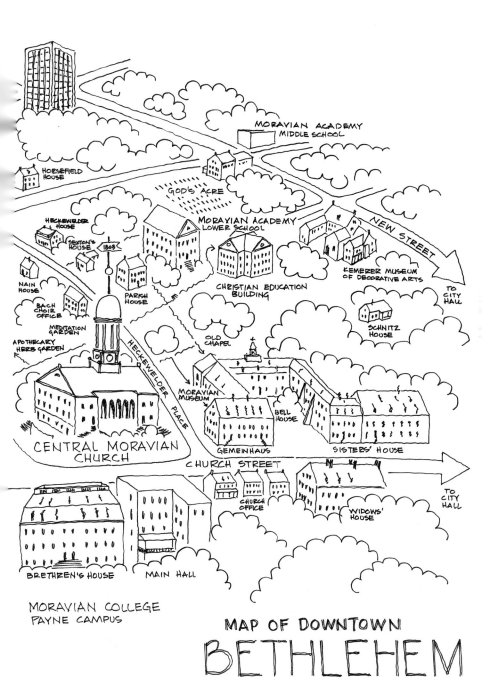

MAP OF DOWNTOWN
BETHLEHEM

Bethlehem, Pennsylvania! You have come to one of the great destinations in the United States of America. It has a long, rich and fascinating story to tell. We have developed this guide book to help your visit be more interesting. As you tour the Moravian campus, we want to help you develop eyes to not only see, but understand what is around you.

The Moravians first came to Bethlehem in 1741. Even though the Moravians were few in number, they have made an inexorable mark in history. Their purpose was to maintain a self-disciplined life which centered around worship, work and mission. Life for these early settlers was devotional, disciplined and viewed as a sacrament. The earliest members lived communally, that is, they dedicated themselves to the development of the community and the church as opposed to any personal gain or aggrandizement.

After a **brief sojourn in the community of Nazareth**, the Moravians purchased 500 acres of land located along the banks of the Lehigh River and Monocacy Creek. In the summer of 1741, a temporary house was built on a site where the Hotel Bethlehem

stands today. One half of the building was used for lodging and the other half served as a stable. On **Christmas Eve, 1741**, the German patron of the Moravians, Count Nikolas Ludwig von Zinzendorf and his daughter, Countess Benigna, officially named the community Bethlehem.

The Gemeinhaus

As the first house of Bethlehem was built, work on another structure also began. It would be known as the Gemeinhaus or **"community house."** Today it is better known as the Moravian Museum. You will want to be sure to see this building and may do so by arranging a guided tour.

The Gemeinhaus is a gray clapboard building. In reality, it is a log structure. Some of the logs have been exposed inside for visitors to see. It is an amazing building in that at first, it housed the entire community. It was a place for worship, education, industry, lodging, dining and government.

The Gemeinhaus is listed as a **National Historic Landmark**. You can see the marker on the southeast corner of the building. It gained this notoriety because of Lewis David deSchweinitz, who was born in the Gemeinhaus and went on to become the first person in America to receive an earned doctorate. He is known as the "Father of Mycology" in America. You will also want to read the large marker next to the steps on the southwest end of the building which describes some of the work of Moravians among the **American Indians** and lists the names of many notable Moravians who lived there.

Another brass marker on the front of the building notes that it was once referred to as the "Clergy House."

The **first place of worship** was located on the second floor of the building in a large room known as the "Saal." Here regular worship services were held and many baptisms also took place including that of Wanab, an American Indian from the Delaware nation.

The Moravians carried out an extensive work among American Indians. They viewed this native population with respect as "the children of God." They sought to Christianize them, educate them and to let them have equal opportunities as those of the European colonists. The efforts touched individuals from the Delaware nation, primarily the Lenni Lenape; Mohegans from New York; some Shawnee; and Cherokee from North Carolina.

Countess Benigna von Zinzendorf established a small **school for girls** in Germantown, PA, and moved it to Bethlehem in June 1742, where the first classes were held in the Gemeinhaus. It would eventually be recognized as the first boarding school for girls in the original 13 colonies. Both Moravian Academy and Moravian College trace their roots of origin to this school.

It is believed that the Gemeinhaus could have been **"America's First Hospital,"** because it is a known fact that a Women's Infirmary and a Men's Dispensary were housed here as early as 1746. Many of the Moravians had been trained in medicine in Europe before coming to America. A pharmacy was also housed here under the direction of Dr. Adolph Meyer. This gave rise to the formation of herb gardens and an apothecary which you will want to see on your visit.

The little street or alley west of the Gemeinhaus is known as **Heckewelder Place**. It is named after the famous missionary, John Heckewelder, who worked among the American Indians. His home is located on the east side of the alley, north of Church Street. Today it is a private residence.

Central Moravian Church

On the corner of Church and Main Streets is the imposing and impressive structure known as Central Moravian Church. It is the **third place of worship** which was begun in 1803 and completed in 1806. When it was dedicated, there were 580 people residing in Bethlehem. Originally designed to accommodate 1500 people, today, because of fixed pews, it seats approximately 1100 people.

It has been suggested that the original plans developed in the 1700's envisioned the construction of such a large church to accommodate not only the Moravians of the community but also the American Indians camped around the village, as well as German settlers who had no other church to attend.

Because of unanticipated delays, actual construction of the church did not begin until 1803. By that time, there were hardly any American Indians living in the area. In the meantime, other churches for the German settlers were constructed. Even though two major factors which inspired the construction of such a large church building no longer existed, the Moravians went ahead with original plans.

As you observe the outside of the church, you will note that it is stucco. This is overlaid on rubble stone. The architectural style is Georgian (named after King George) which following the American Revolutionary War became known as **"Federal Architecture."**

As America began defining itself as a new nation, it wanted to embrace the very best of architectural styles. The Greeks and Romans were recognized as having the most beautiful and enduring architecture. Federal architecture defined itself in part as being neo-classical. Many of these features are exhibited in the Central Moravian Church structure. The corners of the building, the windows and doors define neo-classicism.

The most prominent feature is the stately **belfry** with its clean, symmetrical lines, beautiful columns and green copper dome which is capped with a weather-vane with the 1803 date that signifies the beginning of

10

construction of the building. The weathervane measures over 7 feet across.

The Belfry

The belfry has a bell in it which was made in Troy, New York in 1868. It continues to strike on the hour.

Two smaller bells rest underneath the large bell. They were cast in 1746 by Samuel Powell and used to strike the quarter hour, but no longer do so.

The belfry also features the **oldest running town clock in America**. The 4 clock faces are visible from the ground. They are 5 feet in diameter. The clock hands measure 36½ and 30 ½ inches. The Roman numeral hour numbers are 8 inches high.

The movement of the hands of the clock are dependent upon the clock works housed in a room below the clock faces. The clock works originally resided in the Bell House. Augustine Neisser built the clock works in 1747; it was moved to the church tower upon the completion of construction.

Access to the belfry is very limited. Its most frequent visitors would be members of the Bethlehem Area Moravians Trombone Choir, who go there to announce festival days, as well as deaths of members the last Sunday of each month.

Central Moravian Church is surrounded on three sides (east, west and south) by a **brick wall which is capped with brownstone.** Upon the wall is a weighty Gothic iron fence.

By 1855, it was recognized that the original wall needed to be replaced and plans were begun to design the current profile of the wall and the brownstone steps. The current design remains essentially the same, even though repairs have been made over the years. It is noted in the minutes of the Board of Trustees for December 24, 1855, that there was a desire for the steps, walls and fences to be "of such an appearance, that the eyes of the visitors were immediately favorably impressed with their neat appearance as well as substantiality."

Conspicuous features of the brick wall include a bulge, or pot belly, at the center of the west wall and along the south side on Church Street there are five stepped sections to conform to the sloping hill.

You will want to be sure to see the bronze plaque on this south wall which designates Central Moravian Church as **"A Landmark of American Music."** It notes that the first American performance of Johann Sebastian Bach's *"Mass in B minor"* was performed here on March 27, 1900. Central Moravian Church is the original home of the world renowned **Bach Choir of Bethlehem.**

At night, the church is warmly lit by carriage lights which surround it. The illumination of the church belfry creates a meditative as well as strikingly impressive sight each evening.

Frequently, visitors are interested in the protruding structures on the slate roof. They are "snow catchers" which help to allow snow to melt gradually, rather than cascading off the roof in one piece.

At each of the six entrances into the church are metal appendages which create a curiosity for visitors. They are "boot scrapes" that were used to clean peoples' shoes before entering the church. In all, there are 8 "boot scrapes."

Many people are fascinated by the handles on the church's doors. It is a fisted hand which surrounds a steel bar. It is suggested by some that it symbolizes a hand holding a scrolled piece of music. It is believed that the idea of these unique door pulls were inspired by handles on an iron gate which led to a garden in Herrnhut, Germany.

Door handle

Inside the sanctuary, "Grosser Saal," (or nave) of Central Moravian Church, you will immediately note the expansive nature of the area. There are no visible supports. This is due to the massive **truss system** which spans the distance between the northern and southern stone walls. The truss system holds the ceiling of the sanctuary while it also supports the roof and the church's belfry.

The worship setting also reflects a neo-classical profile. The four Corinthian columns help frame the massive pulpit which itself has smaller stately columns carved on it. The pilasters located between the windows give the appearance that they are supported by the wainscoting. In reality, they are hollow structures which encourage worshippers to lift their eyes upward in a meditative and reflective manner.

Central Moravian Church Interior

picture along with a biographical sketch of each woman.

It is thought that Central Moravian Church was the first church in America to be illumined by **indirect lighting**. The lights are in the coving at the top of the walls and behind the arch of the apse where the pulpit is located.

Some other features you will want to observe include the pew cushions. As the uninitiated squeeze them, it is often thought that they are filled with "straw," "corn husks," or "beans." In reality, it is horsehair.

The **needlepoint chairs** were designed to reflect the acanthus leaves at the top of the Corinthian columns surrounding the pulpit area. Each panel was done by individuals of our church in 1986. Each panel includes the initials of the needle pointer. Behind the panel is a plastic bag which includes samples of the various colored yarn used, as well as a

Upon the pulpit is an **open Bible.** This is an essential practice at Central Moravian Church which dates back to one of the tenets of our church's founder, John Hus, who insisted that the scriptures be written in the language of the worshippers.

The **Möller organ** in the balcony at the west end of the church was originally built in 1954. It went through a major renovation and restoration in 2007. Music has always played a vital role in our church and reflects the Moravians' strong adherence to worshipping God through many forms of musical offerings.

If you are in the balcony you will note a large board which has a listing of all of the organists who have served at Central Moravian Church for more than 200 years. You may also note a piece of rope hanging down the back of the north column in the choir loft. It goes through a hole in the ceiling and extends up to the bell in the belfry. It is a reminder that the ringing of the bell used to occur in this location. Today the bell is immobile and is rung electronically.

If you step behind the arches on both the north and south sides of the church and look at the top of the arches you might be able to see our "church angels" at the top.

Just under the balcony on the first floor are the **West Rooms** which are used for meetings, a library, receptions and coat racks. It is also the staging area from which the lovefeast is served. Baskets of buns are individually wrapped in napkins and trays of coffee are placed on the tables. The coffee is made in the large kitchen in the basement. Mugs are filled with coffee on serving trays which are then brought up to the West Rooms on a "dumb waiter" located between the two rooms.

West Rooms

At the east end of the church, two staircases lead into the **"Kleiner Saal,"** or "little meeting room." It serves as a music room where music is stored in cabinets. The Trombone Choir uses it for rehearsals. Bells for the Bell Choir are stored here. Decorating of beeswax candles with a red paper trim happens here each October. An **1857 Erben organ** is housed here, where an occasional organ recital is given or a hymn sing (*Singstunde*) takes place.

14

Two cabinet doors just south of the Erben organ conceal a special secret door, which, when opened, leads into the original **oriel pulpit** that was once in the main sanctuary at about the same height where it can be seen at the southeast stairway.

Oriel Pulpit

On the walls at the top of both staircases is an **incising which indicates the location of an entrance** which once led to a small balcony on either side of the oriel pulpit in the sanctuary.

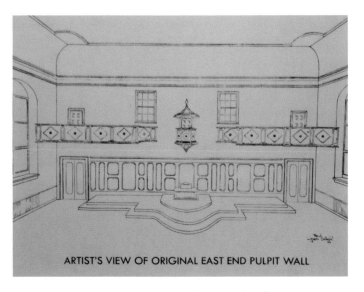

ARTIST'S VIEW OF ORIGINAL EAST END PULPIT WALL

Original Location of the Oriel Pulpit

15

Historical Markers Tell the Story

Within an area a bit larger than a city block, Bethlehem boasts more than 10 historical markers and plaques, placed by the Pennsylvania Historical and Museum Commission. We hope that you will take the time to locate and read them carefully as you explore our city.

Along Market Street:
Pulaski's Banner – at God's Acre Moravian women made a banner for General Casimir Pulaski's cavalry.

Moravian Cemetery – God's Acre Burial place, 1742-1910.

Along Church Street:
Bell House
Site of the first town clock.

Sisters' House
Unmarried women lived, worked and worshipped here.

Gemeinhaus
Count Zinzendorf had his quarters here; Site of the Great Wedding, July 15, 1749.

John Frederick Wolle
A major interpreter of J.S. Bach's music and founder of the internationally known Bach Choir of Bethlehem was born here.

Brethren's House
Unmarried men lived, worked and worshipped here.

Along Main Street:
Moravian Community
Organized June 25, 1742.

Along Heckewelder Place:
Heckewelder House
The first owner was a missionary who wrote books about the American Indians.

Old Chapel
The second place of worship.

The Upper Green

There are a number of interesting sites on the "Upper Green," to the east of Central Moravian Church that you will want to visit.

The Upper Green, Sisters' House on left; Bell House on right

Across Heckewelder Place, the street next to the church, stand several buildings important in the lives of Moravians of the past, as well as in the lives of the students, worshippers and residents today.

Visitors are often surprised to discover that each building is still in active use, some after over 200 years of existence.

Some of the buildings are now private residences.

Gemeinhaus

1741 Gemeinhaus, 66 West Church Street

Known today as the Moravian Museum, the 1741 Gemeinhaus, or 'community house,' is the oldest existing structure in Bethlehem. Part of the second floor contains the 'Saal,' the first place of worship for the Moravians.

Constructed of logs, now covered with clapboard, the Gemeinhaus was the center of the community as a residence and as a gathering place. It has been designated a National Historic Landmark.

Museum hours are Thursday through Sunday, 10 a.m. - 5 p.m. Sunday, noon- 5 p.m. Closed January, February and March.

Please see page 8 for more details.

Old Chapel

Constructed in 1751, the Old Chapel is a favorite place for weddings, concerts and memorial services, and for weekly chapel services for Moravian Academy. The Chapel is used each Sunday, September through May, for the 9 a.m. worship service of Central Moravian Church. Seating is for about 200 people.

Notable figures from colonial days worshiped in the Chapel, including George and Martha Washington, Benjamin Franklin, John Adams, Samuel Adams, John Hancock, Ethan Allen, Count Casimir Pulaski, General Horatio Gates, John Paul Jones and the Marquis de Lafayette.

On March 10, 1792, fifty-one chiefs and representatives of the Six Nations (Iroquois Confederacy) came to Bethlehem on their way to Philadelphia to meet with George Washington. Among them were the great chiefs Red Jacket, Corn Planter and Big Tree. They gathered in the Old Chapel, the Indians in ceremonial feathers and leggings and the brethren and sisters in their plain garb.

The Chapel now has a very simple interior, but in earlier days, oil paintings by the Moravian artist John Valentine Haidt, adorned the walls. The paintings depicted events in the life of Christ.

The Chapel had been in continuous use as the main worship center of the Bethlehem Moravians until the construction of the third place of worship, the sanctuary of Central Moravian Church. Renovated in 1998, and with the addition of a lift, the Old Chapel is fully accessible.

It includes a multi-purpose room in the basement, shared regularly by the Senior High Chat Group and the Busy Workers' Society of Central Moravian Church.

Bell House

The Bell House, facing the Upper Green

A field stone building with a distinctive belfry and weathervane with the Lamb and banner seal, the Bell House connects to the Old Chapel on the west and the Sisters' House on the east.

It was built in 1746 to be a residence for married couples of the early community. Two additions to the building followed, in 1748 and 1749.

Much later, it was used by Moravian Seminary and College for Women. Today it is owned and managed by Bethlehem Area

.

Moravians, Inc., as apartments for couples or individuals.

The belfry contains a bell cast in 1776 by Matthias Tommerup. The clock that was built by Augustine Neisser and installed in the Bell House in 1747 was moved to the belfry of Central Moravian Church.

Although the door between them no longer exists, in colonial days, a church-goer could access the Old Chapel from the second floor of the Bell House without going outdoors.

Sisters' House

At its construction in 1744, this building was designed to serve as the Brethren's House for the community.

When the 'brethren,' the single men, moved to larger quarters on Church Street, the building was given to the single women in 1748 as a residence.

It was also a place for women to learn skills and to carry out their handicrafts. It included a dining area and dormitories.

Little has changed in the interior since the early days of the Sisters' House, except for the addition of electricity, modern plumbing and cable television.

Dormitory living is still available here for single individuals through Bethlehem Area Moravians, Inc.

The Sisters' House – Church Street view facing west

Schnitz House

The 1801 Schnitz House is named for *schnitz*, the sliced, dried apples that were produced and prepared here by the early community.

Today the Schnitz House is a charming private residence.

The Schnitz House, facing West Church Street

Kemerer Museum of Decorative Arts

The home-like atmosphere of this museum provides the setting for treasures from the Victorian era of Bethlehem up to contemporary times.

A recent addition has been the extensive dollhouse collection given to the Museum by Elizabeth Johnston Prime, granddaughter of the first mayor of Bethlehem.

The Kemerer Museum is one of the museums of the Historic Bethlehem Partnership.

Kemerer Museum of Decorative Arts, North New Street

God's Acre

The old cemetery of the Moravians, planned in 1742, is the final resting place for many individuals of the colonial era.

Flat stones, arranged according to the *choir* system, mark the graves of women, men and children, both ordinary and notable people; colonists and converted American Indians. They lie in peace and in equal status before God in what is referred to as the 'democracy of death.'

An American Indian named Tschoop lies here, after whom novelist James Fenimore Cooper fashioned his character Uncas in the book, *The Last of the Mohicans*.

God's Acre was closed to interments in 1912, but continues to be maintained by Bethlehem Area Moravians, Inc.

Visitors often stroll the paths of the cemetery. Moravian Academy students regularly use a part of the open space as a play area.

God's Acre – facing Moravian Academy Middle School

Central Moravian Church
Christian Education Building

The Christian Education Building serves many purposes in the life of the community. It houses part of the Lower School of Moravian Academy, as well as the ongoing Church School and nursery for the Central Moravian Church congregation.

Each year, the lower level of this building is transformed by the presence of the **Christmas *Putz***, a display of lighted figures with audio narration, depicting the Nativity story.

Groups from the larger community meet in its classrooms and halls, including 2 AA groups, AAUW, Amnesty International and others on an occasional basis.

Benigna Auditorium, first floor, is named for Countess Benigna, daughter of Count Zinzendorf. **Nitschmann Hall** is named for David Nitschmann, one of the founders of the community. Count Zinzendorf's portrait hangs in the graciously appointed **Zinzendorf Parlor**, lower level.

Built in 1901, the CE Building has served the church well. In 1966, and again in 1998, significant renovations of the building made it an even more attractive and accessible space.

Christian Education Building – View from God's Acre

Moravian Academy Main Building

View from the Bell House

This structure, built in 1857, is home to the students of the Lower School of Moravian Academy.

The Academy is a private day school with two additiona campuses, one on nearby Market Street, for Middle School students and one at Green Pond in Bethlehem Township for students in the Upper School.

Parish House

Facing the Old Chapel is the Parish House built in 1822 as a boys' school. It is owned by the Bethlehem Area Moravians, Inc., and used as apartment residences.

The previous use of the building was for regular gatherings of groups such as the Starmakers, Ladies' Sewing Society, Friendship Bible Class and Busy Workers' Society of Central Moravian Church.

Parish House
Across from the Old Chapel
(Under Renovation)

Sexton's House

The Sexton's House lies directly behind the Parish House and was built in about 1800.

The sexton of Central Moravian Church resides in the home today.

Sexton's House – View from the Old Chapel

Heckewelder House

The large, private residence located behind the Sexton's House is the John Heckewelder House.

It was named after John Heckewelder, a Moravian missionary who worked among the American Indians in the Ohio territory. George Washington appointed him the first United States Commissioner to the Indians of the Ohio territory after the Revolutionary War.

Built in 1810 as Heckewelder and his wife Susan's retirement home, the home is now owned and managed by Bethlehem Area Moravians, Inc.

Heckewelder Place

The street running between Central Moravian Church and the Old Chapel at the Church Street intersection which is now known as Heckewelder Place was officially named Cedar Street in 1819.

The Parish House, on Heckewelder, was once named the Cedar Street School.

Perpendicular to Cedar Street and next to Central Moravian Church was an alley that no longer exists. It is often shown on the postcards of the day.

On West Church Street

Buildings you will want to identify include the Widows' House, the Central Moravian Church Office Building and the Brethren's House.

Widows' House

Moravian Theological Seminary now owns the 1768 Widows' House, located on West Church Street facing the Bell House/Sisters' House complex.

A later addition on the southwest portion of the building is especially identifiable. The reddish color of the stone used is from the iron ore present in its composition.

Originally planned as a home for widows of clergy and missionaries, the Widows' House is now home to Seminary students and other single or married residents from the Moravian community. The building is not open to the public.

The Widows' House, West Church Street

28

Central Moravian Church Office Building

The Church office building at 73 West Church Street was built in 1831 as the "President's House," for the Provincial Helpers' Conference. Its first resident was Bishop John Daniel Anders. From 1947 – 1985 it served as the **headquarters for the Moravian Church Northern Province.** In 1986, Central Moravian Church purchased the building.

In the fall of 1987, renovations were completed and the building dedicated as the office building for Central Moravian Church. The basement of the building is home to a number of ministries. Here the **Candle Makers** pour beeswax candles for the Christmas Eve services. **Cynthia's Boutique** is a clothing bank from which good, used clothing is distributed to local and regional agencies. The **Food Bank** distributes food once a month to local families and individuals. The **World Imports Shop** sells handcrafted items from around the world. Proceeds benefit the work in Sikonge, Tanzania, East Africa.

Church Office Building, 73 West Church Street

29

Brethren's House

Brethren's House, West Church and Main Street intersection

The Brethren's House, built in 1748, was originally intended as a dormitory-home for 72 single boys and men. It became necessary to expand the structure to accommodate "the weavers and hat makers" in 1768.

On top of the building is a little white picket platform or **"widow's walk,"** where hymn tunes were played to announce the death of individuals belonging to the community, as well as special festival events.

Some believe that on Christmas Day 1755, a group of **hostile American Indians** were ready to attack the village of Bethlehem, when the sound of the trombones being played from the top of the Brethren's House frightened them so much that they fled with the feeling that the "Great Spirit" did not want then to harm the community.

(con't.)

30

The Brethren's House served as a **Continental Army Hospital** twice during the Revolutionary War, from December 4, 1776 to July 21, 1777, and from September 20, 1777 to April 14, 1778. Over 300 soldiers, many Virginians, died here and many Moravian brethren who tended to them also lost their lives from "camp fever."

On September 25, 1782, General George Washington worshipped here in the chapel.

On November 10, 1815, the building became a school for women known as, the **Young Ladies' Seminary.** In 1957, it was consolidated into Moravian College and currently houses offices and classrooms for the Music Department.

The stone lintel on the north side of the building carries an inscription, "May the young men's activity redound to the praise of the Trinity." On the south side of the building is another lintel over the south door with an engraved star and the words, "Gloria Pleura." ("Praise to the [wounded] side."

On the south side of the building the year 1748 is inscribed. There is also a **sun dial** on the building which is considered to be in perfect alignment due to the preciseness of the building.

A set of steps have been added in more modern times to lead up to the doors on the south side. The doors and stairs are purely decorative and not truly functional.

The Church Green

Around 1934, several buildings that were adjacent to Central Moravian Church on its north were demolished to create what we know affectionately as the Church Green. Among those buildings was Simon Rau and Company, considered the oldest drug store in the United States. It was established in 1743.

Today a portion of the building survives as one of the gift shops of the Moravian Book Shop, the Apothecary and private apartments on the second floor.

A rock with a bronze plaque situated on the Church Green indicates that Eugene A. Rau was responsible for providing this open space. This tribute was presented in 1935.

Central Moravian Church

Please see p.10 for details.

Central Moravian Church - from the Hill to Hill Bridge

Moravian Book Shop

The Moravian Book Shop is the oldest book store in America and perhaps in the world.

Established in 1745, it served as a place for the distribution of publications by the Church. It has now expanded into a "Cook Shop," with many fine delectables such as candies, pastries as well as many wonderful selections at its delicatessen.

Moravian Book Shop, Main Street

It abounds as a gift shop and offers Christmas decorations and unique specialty items year round.

Apothecary

The Apothecary, facing the Herb Garden

From Bethlehem's earliest days, one of the first provisions to be made was for the care of the sick. In 1742, an Apothecary was begun in the Gemeinhaus (now the Moravian Museum.)

In 1752, it was moved to its present location at the rear of the Moravian Book Shop, located at 424 Main Street.

On its shelves are 25 Delft jars from Holland for the storage of gums, ointments and resins. Mortars, pestles, a copper pigment scale and clay vessels made by American Indians are on display in this unrivaled space.

Herb Garden

From the earliest days in Bethlehem, Moravians knew of the **medicinal value of herbs**.

They explored the countryside to find plants with healing properties. In recognition of this knowledge and interest, two herb gardens have been developed and maintained.

The "Knot" in the Herb Garden

The first was designed in 1946. It is located on the north side of the Church Green between Main Street and Heckewelder Place.

A conspicuous feature of this "garden on the Green" is a **"knot,"** which is created by miniature boxwoods. The idea of this knot was inspired by a book published in London in 1577 called, "The Gardener's Labyrinth," by Thomas Hill.

The Herb Garden contains samples of many of the herbs which would have been growing in Bethlehem in the 1700's. Other perennials have been added such as geraniums, coral bells, meadow rue and turtle head because they are more tolerant of the shade. The garden also contains miniature daffodils, iris reticulata and tulips which bloom in early Spring.

A second garden was planted behind the Apothecary in 1995. It also contains many examples of historic plants which were known to have been used in the 1752 Apothecary.

Meditation Garden

"Be still and know that I am God..."

The Meditation Garden was developed in 1999 as a quiet resting place for individuals to reflect and meditate. A small stone with a bronze plaque upon it has a reminder from Psalms, "Be still and know that I am God."

A variety of shrubs and plants with white flowers are planted in the garden.

Bach Choir Office

Be sure to see the Bach Choir office building located on Heckewelder Place. The Bach Choir had its origins at Central Moravian Church in 1901. The Bach Choir, currently features the popular *"Bach at Noon"* concerts at Central Moravian Church the second Tuesday of each month between September and April at 12:10 p.m. (except during December.)

The Bach Choir has also featured special significant concerts at Central Moravian Church such as the "Japanese Bach Concerto," and the performance of the 100th Anniversary concert of the *"B minor Mass."*

The Bach Choir Office Building, which wants to remain close to its original roots contains an archives, office space and is the location for retail sales of tickets and CD's.

Nain-Schober House

The term, "American Home," takes on a new meaning as you visit the Nain-Schober House. It was built in 1758 by Moravian missionaries and American Indians in the Village of Nain, which was situated in the western part of Bethlehem. It is the only surviving house from the village.

Perhaps this was due to the decision and efforts of Andreas Schober, who purchased the house in 1765 and moved it to Market Street near Heckewelder Place.

In 1906 it was relocated again, this time to Heckewelder Place. A bronze bust of David Zeisberger adorns the lawn behind the Nain-Schober House. Zeisberger was a Moravian teacher among the American Indians for over 60 years. This rendering of him was presented as a commemorative gift in 1992, as part of the 250th anniversary celebration of the community of Bethlehem.

Today the Nain-Schober House is under the management of the Moravian Museum.

Moravians have always been faithful record keepers. Whether in official minutes of boards and committees, in newsletter articles, in annual reports, or in carefully preserved correspondence, Bethlehem Moravians have captured their history for future generations.

Fascinating glimpses of both day to day life and more extraordinary events in the history of our community can be found in the pages of a church journal dated, June 30, 1940 – December 31, 1952.

Never before published, these entries reflect such things as the sad news of a fire in the sanctuary of Central Moravian Church; the reaction of the community to a declaration of war; the renovation of beloved colonial buildings; the plea for funds for hurricane relief; the poignant dedication of a gift in memory of a soldier who died in service to his country.

We share them with you as a reminder of the life of a vibrant community of faith that existed years ago and that helped to give shape to our community today.

Saturday, November 29th, 1941 – "Fire in the Central Church At 1:30 in the morning, fire was discovered in Central Church. Due to the efficient work on the part of the fire departments, the building was saved, though quite badly damaged. This was a very severe blow, the auditorium having just been redecorated and with the Bicentennial services just a month off."

Headlines of a newspaper article that was attached to the journal declared, "Central Church Fire Damage Set at Near $40,000; - ORGAN IS RUINED"

The article cited the cause of the fire as an overheated motor on the blower of the church's hot air heating system. It was noted that many other local congregations were quick to offer their churches for Central's use.

Sunday, December 7, 1941 – "Japan attacks - Word reached us via radio that Japan has attacked, without warning, a number of our bases in the Pacific. Many casualties are reported. It is expected the President will ask Congress for a declaration of war."

Monday, December 8, 1941 –
"The President of the United States met a joint session of Congress today at 12:30 o'clock and asked for a declaration of war against Japan following the attacks of yesterday. The declaration was passed 43 minutes later by both houses of Congress and at 4:10 this afternoon the act was signed by the President. We are at war."

Thursday, December 11, 1941 –
"Word reached us this morning that Italy and Germany had declared war on the United States. The condition we had hoped to avoid has come.

The signal for an air raid alarm in Bethlehem was announced on the radio this morning. Three blasts repeated three times on the fire alarm system is the signal. The "all clear" is two blasts repeated twice.

May God give us success in this conflict."

Monday, December 22, 1941 –
"The script for the radio broadcast of our vigil services was examined today and approved.

The community hymn sing was held on the Hill to Hill bridge this evening.

Soldiers of the United States Army appeared at different places in Bethlehem today guarding different places in and near the city."

February 24, 1949 – "The remodeling of the Schnitz House which will include the building of an addition to it so that it can be used as a parsonage for the assistant pastor was started on Monday last.

Today there was central heat in the Sisters' House for the first time in its 200 year history."

Palm Sunday, March 18, 1951 - Permanent flood lighting for the belfry was dedicated.
From a letter by C. H. H. Weikel:

"Dear Dr. Allen,
When we came to Bethlehem to live – now more than 30 years ago, the belfry on Central Moravian Church was visible from our apartment. The years that we have lived in this community have but strengthened our first thoughts, that the belfry in its simple beauty stands forth to convey to all who see it, the message of the character of those who built it and worshipped underneath it.
I have thought for several years that the lighting of the belfry should be on a permanent basis so that it could be used at any time during the year and not to be confined to the temporary fixtures used during the Christmas season.

To that end, I would consider it a privilege if I could be allowed to pay for the installation of a permanent lighting system.

We lost our young son, John Hart Weikel in the last war and I would like to think of the gift somewhat as a memorial to him…"

A plaque commemorating this gift reads, in part,

> In memory of
> John Hart Weikel, p.f.c.
> Company "K" 394th Infantry
> 99th Division
> Born Bethlehem, PA
> September 25, 1924
> Wounded in Germany,
> November 23, 1944
> Died Paris, France
> December 3, 1944
> Buried U.S. Military Cemetery
> Epinal, France

December 24, 1951 – an insert in the Christmas Eve Vigil programs read: "The Board of Elders voted to devote the Christmas Eve offering to **Jamaica Hurricane Relief** and to ask for a generous contribution for this emergency.

The Hurricane was the worst in 100 years, left 600 schoolhouses flat, blew down thousands of homes, destroyed churches and ruined all crops. Many of our churches had roofs blown off, windows blown in."

These brief narratives also remind us that life in Moravian Bethlehem did not exist in a vacuum. The world was changing; people's lives were changing.

And in the midst of change, many Moravians found comfort and a sense of hope as they repeated the rituals of the Christian faith that had always sustained them.

Lovefeasts, anniversary celebrations, organ concerts, music festivals and Christmas Eve Vigil services, all became the rich traditions that carried them through the years.

Recent Celebrations

The Central Moravian Church congregation celebrated three anniversaries in close proximity:

❖ the 100th anniversary of the construction of the Christian Education Building in 1901;

❖ the 250th Anniversary of the construction of the Old Chapel in 1751;

❖ the 200th Anniversary of the construction of the Central Moravian Church sanctuary in 1803-1806.

The **200th Anniversary celebration of the construction of the sanctuary** led the congregation of Central Moravian Church to gather items for a **time capsule** to be opened 100 years in the future.

The capsule that was installed in the Southeast corner stairwell of the sanctuary and included:

Peanut Makers - Description of the organization; bags of peanuts and cashews

Busy Workers - List of members; photos and description of the Anna Nitschmann doll; flyer on the Moravian Historical Plates; program from the tea in honor of the 250th anniversary of the Old Chapel; book, *Benigna, the Chapel Mouse*, and stuffed mouse; red velvet pin cushion

Music Committee - Description of the organization and copies of the 2002 programs for the Easter and Christmas Eve services

World Imports Shop - Description of the organization and carved wooden bird

Kitchen Committee - Description of the organization; *Belfry* article

about the new kitchen; tickets for the 2002 Spaghetti Dinner

Food Bank - Brief history

Twenty Minutes Society - Brief history; excerpts from the Society's annual reports from the 1890s

Cynthia's Boutique - Description of the clothing bank

Christian Education Committee - Booklet, *Celebrating the 100th Anniversary of the Christian Education Building, 1901-2001*

Friendship Bible Class - Brief history

Stewardship Committee - Pledge card, offering envelopes, and booklet on the 2003 budget

Tape Ministry - Brief description and example of a mailing to out-of-town or shut-in members

Moravian Women - Directory, photographs, and recipes for chicken pie and sugar cake

Social Action Committee - Statement of purpose, reports, minutes, and agendas of

40

selected meetings and programs, 2001-2003

Handbell Choir - Description and list of members, music, and pair of white gloves

Senior High Chat Group - "Listen Up," a compact disk with favorite songs of members of the Chat Group

2003 and 2006 Confirmation Class - Essays and messages to the future

Photograph album - Central congregation and church campus

Christmas in Bethlehem: A Moravian Heritage by Vangie Roby Sweitzer, 2000. Inscribed by the author.

200th Anniversary Keepsake calendar, 2005

Old Chapel 250th anniversary - Married Couples Reunion, May 19, 2002 - Sketches and photographs of decorations

Sikonge Committee - description of committee and container of rice given to Central as a "thank offering" by John Kifutumo, pastor of the Sikonge Moravian Church

Ladies Sewing Society - History, samples of materials for making Polly Heckewelder dolls, transcript of interview with Alice Knouss about the doll making, April 2, 2003

Central Moravian Annual Report, 2005

Outreach and Evangelism Committee - "Welcome to Central" DVD and transcript, "Welcome to Central" brochure, visitor's welcome packet

"Central Moravian Church" supplement to the *Morning Call*, April 30, 2006 "Music at Central, 2005-06" brochure

"Moravian Days, 2006" flyer

Pictorial Directory of Central Church, 2005

Tuned for Praise: The Bethlehem Area Moravian Trombone Choir, 1754-2004 by Vangie Roby Sweitzer, 2004.

"Dennis the Menace Visits the Christmas City" by Hank Ketcham and Fred Toole - Comic book reprint, 2005

Brownstone Steps Capital "Central Church: A Prism of Faith" by Barbara Caldwell, talk given on May 6, 2006; "Historic Moments" by Barbara Caldwell, 2003-2006

A History of Central's Sanctuary DVD, presented at the worship service, May 7, 2006

Historic Bethlehem Partnership - Moravian Museum "candle in the window" tile by Starbuck Goldner

Campaign brochure, 2005 Moravian Academy - Parent Directory, 2005-2006 and list of faculty and staff members

Moravian College - College and Seminary catalogs, brochures, scarf, and college seal glass paperweight

City of Bethlehem - Citation in recognition of the 200th Anniversary; city pin; Mayor Callahan's card, photograph, and 2006 "State of the City" presentation; "Bethlehem: It's Happening Here" CD

Advent

The Advent season, four weeks preceding Christmas, is marked with preparations of all kinds. An Advent **Lovefeast** is held in the sanctuary of Central Moravian Church at 11 a.m. on the first Sunday of Advent. During the partaking of the lovefeast, the choir sings anthems relating to the season. There is no sermon; the message of preparation and hope is conveyed through the singing by the congregation and choir.

As you step inside the Christian Education Building a bit earlier on Advent Sunday, the sights, sounds and spicy aromas of the season greet you at the traditional **Advent Workshop**. Children and adults enjoy crafts, cookie-baking and visiting the Christmas **Putz**.

Candles are seen in every window during the season, a tradition of German Moravians of the 1700's.

Lighted Moravian stars shine from doorways, reminding us of the star that once led the wise men to the Christ Child. The star, first made as a school project in Germany, is a 26 pointed star that is displayed throughout the season.

Christmas

In her book, *Christmas in Bethlehem*, author Vangie Sweitzer writes, "Each December, many thousands come to Bethlehem from all over the world to be moved by the heritage and traditions, to experience what has become known as Christmas City, USA and to share in the sights and sounds of a city steeped in three centuries of history."

The beauty and meaning of the season is captured in the 3 Christmas Eve services at Central Moravian Church. The Children's Lovefeast, the 5:30 p.m. and 8 p.m. Vigils are all candle services, with each worshipper receiving a lighted beeswax candle, signifying that Christ is the light of the world.

Sanctuary at Christmas

New Year's Eve

The congregation at Central Moravian Church gathers for worship in the sanctuary at 11:30 p.m.

At the stroke of midnight, the Bethlehem Area Moravians Trombone Choir begins to play, interrupting the pastor's sermon. The pastor reads the *Daily Text* for the new day and offers prayer for the coming year.

Epiphany

The Epiphany season is celebrated first with a service of Holy Communion and the following Sunday, with a Lovefeast. A mission speaker is often invited to speak, in keeping with the epiphany theme.

Lent

Ash Wednesday and the Lenten season bring with them an emphasis on enrichment, worship and study. A midweek series emphasizes topics related to this time of preparation for the celebration of Easter.

The days of Holy Week are marked by services at which the *Readings for Holy Week* are offered without interpretation.

The *Crucifixion Service* on Good Friday afternoon includes sung portions of *St. Matthew's Passion.* The *Great Sabbath Lovefeast* on Saturday afternoon is a respite from the sorrow of Good Friday and a foretaste of Easter joy.

Easter

The Trombone Choir begins its traditional trek around the city, playing chorales proclaiming the resurrection of Christ.

The Easter Dawn service begins in the sanctuary of Central Moravian Church and concludes in God's Acre as the sun rises.

The 11 a.m. Triumph Service is a true celebration, with brass and tympani accompanying choir and congregation.

Sanctuary with Lily Cross

Two Unique Times of Remembrance for Moravians

The Moravian Church celebrates Holy Communion on the days of the Church Year common to most Protestant denominations.

We practice **open communion**, which means that members of all Christian Churches are invited to share the bread and the cup of Holy Communion. The form in which the Holy Communion is administered in the Moravian Church differs from that of other churches, for it is based upon practices which began in our church in the 15th century.

The bread and the cup are brought to the pews by one of the pastors, symbolically reminding us of God's initiative through Christ, in coming to each one of us.

There are two unique, additional occasions on which Moravians partake of Holy Communion. Both are in remembrance of important events in the life of the Moravian Church.

On **August 13th**, 1727, the community at Herrnhut, Germany celebrated Holy Communion at a Lutheran Church in nearby Berthelsdorf.

A powerful spiritual experience during that worship caused the fledgling community to set aside theological differences, to learn to love one another and to begin to set themselves the goal of reaching out to those who needed to hear the Gospel of Christ.

The date has become known as the **Spiritual Birthday of the Renewed Moravian Church** and is celebrated with Holy Communion and often with a Lovefeast.

The congregation of Central Moravian Church joins in Holy Communion in the church sanctuary and then processes outdoors for a lovefeast luncheon on the Green.

On the Sunday nearest **November 13th**, we remember that on this date in 1741, the announcement was made that Christ was chosen to be Chief Elder of the Moravian Church. No human being could hold this office; Christ himself was declared to be our leader.

Seal of the Moravian Church

46

A Community Embraces Its History

How do we tell the Bethlehem story most effectively today? Who helps to coordinate the various museums that both display artifacts dating from the 1700's through today and interpret our history?

The **Historic Bethlehem Partnership**, was formed in 1993 to accept this challenge. The Partnership includes the Moravian Museum, founded in 1939 and housed in the Gemeinhaus; Kemerer Museum of Decorative Arts on New Street, 1954; Historic Bethlehem Inc., 1957; and Burnside Plantation, 1986, to the west of the downtown off of Schoenersville Road. The Colonial Industrial Quarter is included in the Partnership. Those buildings are the 1761 Tannery; the 1869 Luckenbach Mill; the 1750/1761 Smithy; and **the 1762 Waterworks**, which is a **National Historic Landmark**.

The Partnership is one of the 139 affiliate members of the Smithsonian Institution and a founding member of the **International Moravian Heritage Network.** The organization unites a worldwide group of representatives from 6 countries and from agencies such as UNESCO.

It is estimated that about 50,000 people visit the museums of the Partnership each year and 16,000 school students.

Purchase tickets and pick up information about special events at the **Welcome Center**, 501 Main Street. Open Tuesday through Saturday, 10 a.m. to 5 p.m.; Sunday, noon to 5 p.m.

Bethlehem Area Moravians, Inc.

The Bethlehem Area Moravians grew from the **Moravian Congregation of Bethlehem**. The congregation was comprised of three local churches: Central, College Hill and West Side Moravian Churches. At one point, Edgeboro Moravian Church was also a member of the Congregation.

Members of the Congregation regularly celebrated Christmas Eve, Children's Lovefeast, Easter Dawn and Anniversary Lovefeast together. The organization was governed by General Elders and General Trustees, whose responsibilities paralleled local elders and trustees.

Recognizing that this old Congregational structure was limiting to the 3 churches that were a part of it, plans were initiated to expand the organization to all 6 Bethlehem Moravian Churches.

The anniversary year of 1992 and the year following, witnessed the advent of Bethlehem Area Moravians, Inc. The **250ᵗʰ Anniversary of Moravians in Bethlehem** both celebrated the past and looked to the future. From this date on, Bethlehem Area Moravians included Advent, Central, College Hill, East Hills, Edgeboro, and West Side Moravian Churches.

A Board of Directors governs the organization; a Ministries Committee is given the mandate to develop cooperative ministries among the churches.

BAM is always seeking ways to better serve and minister to people in the Bethlehem community, especially through **housing**.

BAM owns and oversees a majority of the buildings in the section bounded by Church, Main, Market and New Streets. A 'Common Grounds' agreement was developed among Central Moravian Church, BAM, Moravian Academy and the Moravian Museum to share in the cost for the maintenance and upkeep of the historic campus.

> *BAM is always seeking ways to better serve and minister to people in the Bethlehem community, especially through housing.*

Through its **Partners in Ministry Grants Program**, the Ministries Committee has supported such causes as transportation assistance for Lehigh Valley Moravians traveling to the Gulf Coast for hurricane relief; the Orphans' Program of the Sikonge, Tanzania area; Northeast Moravian Disaster Response Program and others.

Nisky Hill Cemetery on Market Street is owned by Bethlehem Area Moravians, Inc.

Moravian Houses I, II, III and IV are owned and operated by Moravian Development Corporation and provide housing for different populations of the community. Houses I, II and III are available for those of a specific income level; Moravian House IV on North Street is for those who are emotionally challenged, but who can benefit by living in a group home setting.

A continuing care retirement community, **Moravian Village, Inc.** was sponsored initially by Bethlehem Area Moravians, Inc. Its cottages to the south of Market Street and its apartments to the north of Market Street, off of Wood Street, provide secure and comfortable living for older residents.

The Congregations of the Bethlehem Area Moravians

Six local congregations offer different opportunities for followers of Christ to worship, study, serve and enjoy fellowship together. Each church governs itself through official boards and is a part of the Moravian Church, Northern Province, Eastern District. The photos on the following pages show the diversity of settings of these six churches.

More information about these churches, plus telephone numbers and website addresses are listed in the 'Contact Us' section.

Jablonski Seal Found on Bethlehem Area Moravian Buildings

This seal was designed by architect John P. Pharo of Bethlehem from an original seal affixed to the episcopal ordination certificate of David Nitschmann, dated June 14, 1735 and signed by Daniel Ernest Jablonski, grandson of John Amos Comenius, Bishop of the Ancient Unitas Fratrum. The ordination took place in Berlin, March 13, 1735, and this was the transmission of the episcopacy from the old church to the renewed Moravian Church.

The Latin words mean, "Our Lamb has conquered, let us follow him."

The seal can be found on Bethlehem Area Moravian churches and institutions.

Advent Moravian Church

3730 Jacksonville Road   *organized December 25, 1862*

Central Moravian Church

West Church and Main Streets   *organized June 25, 1742*

College Hill Moravian Church

72 West Laurel Street   *organized December 11, 1887*

East Hills Moravian Church

1830 Butztown Road   *organized June 9, 1957*

Edgeboro Moravian Church

645 Hamilton Avenue *organized October 25, 1914*

West Side Moravian Church

402 Third Avenue *organized May 6, 1860*

Moravian Houses I, II, and III - *view from Conestoga Street*

Moravian House IV – North Street

53

Moravian Village Cottages — *facing south, off of Market St.*

Individual Cottage

Moravian Village Apartments — Wood Street

Moravian Village Health Care Center

Scavenger Hunt for Children

1. Find the 8 **boot scrapes** outside the doors of Central Moravian Church.

2. Where is the window that is **not a window** on the Heckewelder Place side of the Church?

3. Read about **American Indians** who met in the Old Chapel on the sign outside the Chapel door.

4. Look for the 'ice cream cones' in the curved window at the peak of the **Old Chapel**.

5. Find **2 maps** of the Church campus – one near the Christian Education Building Parking lot and the other near Main Street.

6. Find the **lamb seal** on the front of the Christian Education Building. *Hint*: look up high!

7. Read the sign on Church Street in front of the Sisters' House. Whose **banner** did the sisters make?

8. Read the printing on the rock in the **Meditation Garden** on the Lower Green. Where did these words come from?

9. Look for the large flat, stone, right in the pathway in God's Acre.

10. What color is the Schnitz House?

A Glossary of Moravian Terms

BAM – The acronym for Bethlehem Area Moravians, Inc. An organization of 6 Bethlehem congregations with a Board of Directors that administers common resources and implements shared ministries.

Choir system – A means of grouping people during the colonial period. There was a single sister's choir; a brethren's choir; a married couples' choir, etc. People lived, worked and worshipped together according to their *choirs.*

Gemeinhaus – The German word for 'Community House.' The Gemeinhaus was the center of life for early Moravians.

General Economy – A plan introduced by Augustus Spangenberg in the 1700s for Bethlehem and Nazareth. The plan was to create a 'community of labor,' but allowed for private ownership of land. People donated their work in exchange for food, clothing and shelter; the Church controlled the products of their work. (1742-1762)

Lovefeast – A simple 'meal' of a lovefeast bun or cookie and a beverage, shared in the context of a worship service. Based upon the *agapē* meal of the early Christian Church, it was reintroduced by the Renewed Moravian Church in the 1700's. It is celebrated today for any number of occasions in the life of a congregation.

Putz – From the German, *putzen* to 'decorate' or to 'clean.' The Central Moravian Church Putz is a display of small figures with special lighting and a taped narration of the story of the birth of Christ. The story of the founding of Bethlehem, PA is also included in the narration.

Schnitz – The cut, dried apples that were a staple of the Bethlehem diet. The Schnitz House is where the apples were dried.

Other Reading to Explore

These books can be purchased at the Central Moravian Church office, 73 West Church Street, Bethlehem, PA :

- ❖ *Christmas In Bethlehem: A Moravian Heritage* by Vangie Roby Sweitzer
- ❖ *Church Street in Old Bethlehem* by Kenneth G. Hamilton; edited and updated by Bernard Michel and illustrated by Fred Bees.
- ❖ *Tuned for Praise: The Bethlehem Area Moravian Trombone Choir, 1754 – 2004* by Vangie Roby Sweitzer.

Other books of interest are:
- ❖ *A History of Bethlehem, 1741-1892,* by Joseph Mortimer Levering
- ❖ *An Architectural History of the Moravian Church* by Garth Howland
- ❖ *Bethlehem of Pennsylvania*, Bethlehem Chamber of Commerce
- ❖ *Christmas Traditions*, by Richmond E. Meyers
- ❖ *History of the Renewed Moravian Church, The Renewed Unitas Fratrum, 1722-1957* by J. Taylor Hamilton and Kenneth G. Hamilton

Moravian Archives

Be sure to visit the **Moravian Archives**, 41 W, Locust Street. The Archives is a wonderful repository of documents, books, maps, paintings and photos of the history of the Moravian Church in America, Northern Province.

Open Monday through Friday, 8 a.m. to 4:30 p.m.

Index

Contact Us

Churches

Advent Moravian Church
3730 Jacksonville Road
Bethlehem, PA 18017
610-866-1402
www.adventmoravianchurch.com

Central Moravian Church
73 West Church Street
Bethlehem, PA 18018
610-866-5661
office@centralmoravianchurch.org
www.centralmoravianchurch.org
Christian Education Building: 610-867-2996
Old Chapel: 610-694-0200

College Hill Moravian Church
72 West Laurel Street
Bethlehem, PA 18018
610-867-8291
www.collegehillmoravian.org

East Hills Moravian Church
1830 Butztown Road
Bethlehem, PA 18017
610-868-6481
www.easthillsmc.org

Edgeboro Moravian Church
645 Hamilton Avenue
Bethlehem, PA 18018
610-866-8793
www.edgeboromoravian.org

West Side Moravian Church
402 Third Avenue
Bethlehem, PA 18018
610-865-0256
   www.westsidemoravian.org

Bethlehem Area Moravians

Bethlehem Area Moravians, Inc.
1021 Center Street
Bethlehem, PA 18017
610-866–1841

Moravian Houses I, II, III, IV
737 Main Street
Bethlehem, PA 18018
610-691-8409

Moravian Village
526 Wood Street
Bethlehem, PA 18018
610-625-4885
   www.moravianvillage.com

Moravian Denomination

Moravian Archives
41 West Locust Street
Bethlehem, PA 18018
610-866-3255
Dr. Paul Peucker, Archivist
   www.moravianchurcharchives.org

Moravian Book Shop
428 Main Street
Bethlehem, PA 18018
610-866-5481
   www.moravianbookshop.com

Moravian Church, Northern Province
1021 Center Street
Bethlehem, PA 18016-1245
610-867-7566
www.mcnp.org

Institutions

Historic Bethlehem Partnership
459 Old York Road
Bethlehem, PA 18018
610-882-0450
Charlene Donchez Mowers,
Executive Director
www.historicbethlehem.org

Moravian Academy Lower School
Heckewelder Place
Bethlehem, PA 18018
610-868-8571
www.moravian.k12.pa.us

Moravian Academy Middle School
11 West Market Street
Bethlehem, PA 18018
610-866-6677

Acknowledgements

Our photographer, Linda Wickmann, deserves special credit for 'going the extra mile' in taking the many wonderful photographs that made this book possible, and by assisting in the design process.

Linda is a native of Ohio. She works currently at East Hills Moravian Church as an administrative assistant. She is married to David Wickmann, President of the Northern Province of the Moravian Church. She and David have 4 children and 2 grandchildren.

Linda's line of greeting cards and note cards are available at Central Moravian Church's Star and Candle Shoppe. You may contact her at lilypad148@verizon.net.

Special thanks to Central Moravian Church member, **Jim Whildin**, for creating the map of Bethlehem. Jim is a partner in the Spillman Farmer Architects. He is also the current President of Historic Bethlehem Partnership, Inc.

Many thanks to **Bethlehem Area Moravians, Inc., Ministries Committee** for generously providing a grant for the publication of this book.

Rick Knapp, Vice President of Chernay Printing Co. has been especially helpful and supportive of the project and has facilitated a wonderful working relationship with his company.

We thank **Barbara Caldwell, Janel Rice, Craig Larimer** and **Paul Peucker** for their invaluable help and guidance.

About the Authors

The Rev. Dr. Douglas W. Caldwell has served Central Moravian Church since 1983. A native of Charlotte, North Carolina, Doug came to Bethlehem in 1964 to attend Moravian College, where he earned a Bachelor's Degree and then continued at Moravian Theological Seminary, where he earned the Master of Divinity degree. He received the Doctor of Ministry Degree from Drew Theological Seminary.

As Senior Pastor, Doug has special responsibilities in church administration and in worship, as well as in overseeing the multiple staff ministry of Central Moravian Church.

Doug is a founding member of the Bethlehem Area Moravians, Inc. and has served on the Board of Directors since its inception. He was one of the founders of Moravian Village, Inc. He is the past Chairman of the Board of St. Luke's Hospital and Health Network, and is a member of the Board of Trustees of Moravian College.

He and his wife, Barbara, are parents of two adult children.

The Rev. Carol A. Reifinger has served Central Moravian Church since August of 1984. She graduated from Liberty High School in Bethlehem in 1965. After receiving her degree in Secondary Education at Kutztown University, she graduated from Moravian Theological Seminary in Bethlehem, PA with a Master of Divinity degree.

Carol's primary focus at Central Moravian Church is in the area of Christian Education, with general pastoral responsibilities as well.

She is one of the founders of the Bethlehem Area Moravians Ministries Committee, of which she currently serves as the Chair. She was one of the founders of Moravian Village, Inc. She is also a member of the Alumni Board of Moravian Theological Seminary. She and her husband, James, are parents of two adult sons.

As A Team

Carol and Doug have championed many causes, such as housing for the homeless, the elderly and the mentally challenged; women's rights; HIV/AIDS in America and Africa; and have been advocates for making churches and public buildings accessible.